BE PREPARED
NOT SURPRISED

by
Peter J. D'Arruda

AUTHOR: Peter J. D'Arruda, CSA, CEA, CCA, CAC

LAYOUT : H. Donald Kroitzsh

Published by:
Financial Safari Press
1135 Kildaire Farm Road
Suite 200
Cary, North Carolina 27512

Telephone: (919) 657-4201
Website: www.FinancialSafari.com
Email: Pete@FinancialSafari.com

Prepared by:
Five Corners Press
Plymouth, Vermont 05056

Printed and bound in the United States of America

Financial Safari — Be Prepared, Not Surprised
ISBN-10: 0-9777993-0-1   US$24.^{95}
ISBN-13: 978-0-9777993-0-5

DEDICATION

This book dedicated to my family:

My loving wife, **Kimberley**, my amazing daughter **Caroline**, and 3 dedicated and always loyal miniature Daschunds, ***Penny, Chelsey, and Allie***, who never have a bad day and are always there when you need someone to talk to.

iv

ACKNOWLEDGMENTS

The process of writing a book at first glance, appears to be an individual project, but the reality is if you want it to be read by thousands or even millions of people, it takes a more than one person to have a finished product to be proud of. I'd first like to thank my wife Kimberley for being so supportive in this process. Without Kimberley, this book would have still just been a dream of mine. Kimberley helped me more than I can ever put into words. She is always there for me and never demands special recognition and is happy to be in the background. She is the oil to my motor and without her, nothing in my life would have ever come close to the levels we have already reached together. A special note of thanks must also be given Kimberley for giving me such a beautiful child in Caroline. Caroline, I look forward to sharing my thanks with you when you reach the age where you can understand what your daddy is saying.

Thanks also to my mother, Dorothy for acting as a mini focus group for me and allowing me to call her for her opinions on topics that were most important to her. My Father, Dr. Jose D'Arruda, for sharing with me various concerns that he has thought of as he nears retirement. Having a close relationship with one's parents is something that should be cherished for supplying memories that will never grow old.

I would also like to thank Dr. Kay Campbell and Mr. Jimmy N. Campbell (Kimberley's parents) for all their support the last 14 years. My relationship with them when I was dating Kimberley, as well as after we were married in 1998, could not be any better if I wrote a script. If everyone had in-laws such as them, the world would be a less violent place.

Special thanks to my publisher, Five Corners Press who have gone the extra mile in this process, and I hope it is apparent in the finished product just how much they have done to insure that the finished product will be a prized and valuable possession to be kept on the top shelf of everyone's bookcase.

TABLE OF CONTENTS

INTRODUCTION

We have all heard the sayings about opinions... To make a long story short – everyone has one. This book is a collection of mine as they apply to the Financial World.

It is important to remember that no one, no matter how smart they claim to be, and no matter what luck they have had in the past, has a crystal ball into the future. Thus, success comes down to:

- Trust in yourself.
- Trust in your Financial Professional.
- Trust in the Government.
- Trust in your family.
- Keep greed to a minimum.
- Aim for consistent returns
- Don't take foolish and (in most cases) unnecessary risks.

Investment and savings decisions ultimately lie with the person who makes them. One of the main aspects of the decision making process is the decision itself. Were the decisions made for the right reasons? Why did you choose to do what you did and would you do it again? Were proper risk planning and risk diversification considered to the fullest extent? Does your current situation meet your risk tolerance? Are fees under control?

Why does it seem we are always being bombarded with supposed gurus screaming their heads off for us to buy this or buy that investment, stock, mutual fund, etc., but they are never around when that advice goes South?

What makes it so acceptable to pay fees for advice that is so wrong? How do some of these companies and advisors get away with this year after year? When will the average investor finally slam their fist down and exclaim they have had enough?

I think of our financial world as a giant glistening onion, and this book is designed to help peel that onion for you, saving you the future tears. I hope it can enable you to make informed decisions which benefit YOU and not the person who is pushing you in a direction that maybe you should not be going, just because they will benefit from your decision. For some of you, this book will be the first real in depth look into your past, present  and future financial situation. For others, this will be the second opinion you have so desperately sought. If you learn through reading this book you are not as prepared as you thought, take action now to correct the situation.

I learned in preschool that square pegs did not fit in round holes. So why is it that as we get older, more and more of us are approached by someone trying to do just that as it relates to our financial port-

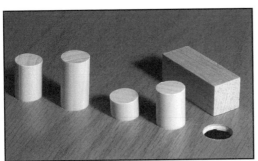

folios? Next time you feel you are being pushed in a direction that you do not feel 100% comfortable with, take a stand and say, "NO!" After all, as many of us witnessed in the market crashes of the years 2000 and 2001, when we lose money, no one magically appears to replace that money.

It is an alarming fact in America today that as life expectancies continue to rise, the savings rate is going in the opposite direction. As we live longer, we must have assets that will live with us. The worst time to learn this fact is upon drawing out the last of our money from the bank. What happens next? The Government will take care of you? Sure they may help but will that "help" enable you to continue to live as you are accustomed? Probably not.

That is why it is especially important to make sure at least some of your savings are placed in vehicles that cannot lose the principal. In addition, you should also have some money in pension-type accounts that promise to pay you an income stream for as long as you live, no matter how long that may be.

Remember, the worst time to discover your financial house was not on a proper foundation is after an unfavorable financial event. Do not let procrastination and misrepresentations rob you of a bright financial future. *Be prepared, not surprised.*

Being prepared is very important with everything in life but never more imperative than when it comes to your financial situation. Hopefully, by taking some time to go through this book and taking an honest and thoughtful look at your situation, you will be ready for any type of financial environment that could develop in the future. The phrase "Be prepared, not surprised" should take on a new meaning.

Simple Rules of Diversification

W hen we get in our car to take a drive somewhere, we are comforted to know that wherever we go, we will have a plethora of road signs warning us about potential pitfalls ahead.

Unfortunately, there are no such signs in the investment world. When did the waters of diversification become so muddy? When is the last time you saw one of these:

There was a time when the meaning of "diversification" was very clear: Having all your eggs in one basket is not a good thing — especially as you age. The older you get, the fewer eggs you should have in the "risk" basket.

The purpose of diversification is to make sure that some of your families' assets are in places where they are protected from inherent risk of the market. Easier said than done these days, especially with all the hype surrounding the Stock Market.

Having money in the bank or in fixed or fixed Index annuities, while not as exciting as the roller coaster ride we call the Stock Market, will keep your money safe, protect it from fluctuating daily, and protect your principal from risk and abuse.

Places where one can have unnecessary risk are the "Wall Street" basket, which includes such things as:

- Stocks
- Bonds
- Mutual Funds
- Limited Partnerships
- Real Estate
- Variable Annuities

Investing all your assets in the basket with these options may initially seem like diversification, and you may actually be told by some people who claim to be financial planners that this is diversification. However, the result is actually financial suicide because all of these options contain the same element – RISK. After all, do twenty eggs in one basket equal diversification? No, but it could make for an awfully large omelet.

Now, no one has the same risk tolerance. Risk tolerance is the amount of risk someone can take before they reach the emotional and financial breaking point. Some cannot stand to lose a penny. Others, seemingly with no pulse, can lose most, if not all, their money and not blink an eye.

The theory is the older you are, the less risk you should take. Younger people can afford more risk because they can go out and get a second job or work overtime to replace the money they lose if undue risks lead to unsightly losses. Most retired people, however, do not want to go out and start working again just to replace the retirement income they need to survive. As a result, most would agree that less risk is very important as you age.

Some risk is acceptable. Keep in mind, however, that there are no guarantees that the more risk you take, the higher your return potential could be; unfortunately, many have found the direct opposite to be true. Thus, it is important not to take overly aggressive chances, to practice proper asset protection, and to help your money help you.

When considering an investment, always ask yourself the following questions:

- **WHY** is this a good investment for me?
- **WHAT** is the potential downside?
- **HOW** can I get out if I want to?
- **WILL** my principal be protected?
- **WHERE** is my money going?
- **WHO** benefits from this investment the most – my family or the salesperson's family?
- **WHEN** do I need this money?
- **HOW** will it pay me back the rest of my life?
- **WHAT** percentage of the investment is at risk?
- **WHY** are big words being used? Are they being used to hide something?
- **WHAT** are the fees?
- **HOW** do the fees affect my return?
- **WHAT** am I not being told?

WHY should someone my age be in the recommended investment?

If you can answer each of these questions with an answer that is acceptable to you, and you still feel good about the particular investment, than maybe it is a good thing for you.

Once you have considered whether a particular investment is good for you, you must determine how much you want to invest. As stated above, your age is often a determining factor in deciding your level of risk. Many people use the following formula to determine the maximum amount they should have at risk:

What is the Right Amount of Risk for You?

100 – Your Age = Maximum Amount of Risk

Here is an example:

Example
Female, age 67
100 – 67 = 33%

In the example above, the female should have 33% of her assets, at most, at risk in ANY type of risky investment. This is because, if this female were to lose the entire 33% she had at risk, she would still be able to live close to her current standard of living. Yes, it would be tough, but at least 67% of her assets would be in a safe place, assuming she had

followed the advice of her Financial Professional and diversified her portfolio.

It does not take a genius to figure out that too much money at risk could put your hopes of a worry-free retirement in danger. As a result, now is the time to make sure YOUR financial plan involves vehicles where your principal is safe and not subject to the risk of the marketplace.

Now, use the formula to figure out the maximum amount you and your spouse should have at risk.

You:

$$100 - \underline{\hspace{2cm}}_{\textbf{(Your Age)}} = \underline{\hspace{2cm}} \%$$

Your Spouse:

$$100 - \underline{\hspace{3cm}} = \underline{\hspace{3cm}} \%$$
$$\text{(Spouse's Age)}$$

Exit Strategy

You hear a lot about exit strategies on the news as it relates to wars and battles. However, the type of exit strategy that is talked about less often, but the one that is the most important for YOU to have, is an **investment exit strategy**.

When you have an investment exit strategy, you decide when you will get out of an investment BEFORE you make the investment. Knowing when you are going to get out before you get in enables you to have a clear head and not have your judgment affected by human nature-type factors, such as greed. Having an exit strategy will insure that you do not lose all your money on a bad investment and

it will also mean you will be able to lock in profits on good investment.

As the story goes, while sitting under an apple tree Sir Isaac Newton was beaned by a falling apple.

Pondering what had just happened, he discovered the Law of Universal Gravity. From this discovery, the popular phrase "What goes up, must come down" was coined.

As the stock market has reached an historic high, you should ponder the practical words of Sir Isaac Newton. Financial planners have long understood that as quickly as the stock market can go up, it can also go down, which it why an exit strategy is so important. Having an exit strategy will help you protect your principal investment.

In planning for your investment exit strategy, here are some questions to ask yourself before investing:

▲ **WHY** am I investing now?

▲ **WHAT** is the target exit price for this investment if it goes up?

- **WHAT** is the target exit price for this investment if it goes down?
- **HOW** much can I afford to lose?
- **HOW** much do I hope to gain in this investment?
- **WHO** is giving me this advice?
- **WHEN** will the next Bear Market hit?

Trust is the key factor when making investment decisions and when planning your exit strategies. Only follow the advice of people you trust. However, even if someone you trust recommends a particular investment, if there is something about the investment that does not feel right, get out of that investment or, better yet, do not even get into it in the first place.

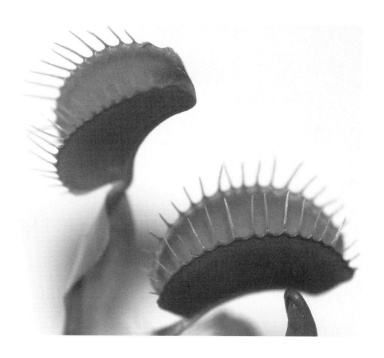

Financial Planning Fundamentals: More than Just Saving and Investing

Financial Planning is a big buzz word these days. Everyone knows they should have a sound financial plan, but what does that really mean and how do you go about getting one?

Let's start out by debunking the myth that a financial plan is nothing more than a smart investment strategy. That is a very narrow view of financial planning. Though extremely important, investing wisely is just one part of a sound financial plan.

To understand the broader concept, think of a financial plan as a roadmap for your finances. With proper and complete planning, this roadmap will take you all the places you want to go, whether that is maintaining a current, comfortable lifestyle; providing your children with an excellent education; or maintaining a nice standard of living in retirement. You may also have a goal of leaving an inheritance to the important people in your life.

The question is how to develop a plan that will enable you to meet all of your goals. The answer is simple: develop a financial plan that does two things:

1. Guards against uncertainty.
2. Grows your investments.

To understand how these objectives fit together, look at this financial planning pyramid.

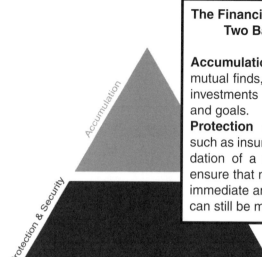

The Financial Pyramid Consists of Two Basic Components

Accumulation Products, such as mutual finds, 401(k) plans, and other investments help fund future plans and goals.

Protection & Security Products, such as insurance, serve as the foundation of a financial plan and help ensure that no matter what happens, immediate and future financial needs can still be met.

Think of the bottom as the foundation of your financial plan. You want to make sure that no matter what twists and turns life sends your way - losing a job, becoming sick or disabled, living too long, or dying too soon – you will have a financial safety net in place to protect you and your family. This foundation is comprised of assets like insurance and emergency savings.

The top part of your pyramid is the asset accumulation component of your plan. Your investment decisions will hopefully fund all of the dreams and ambitions you have for you and your family. This part of the pyramid consists of appreciating assets like stocks, bonds, mutual funds, and college and retirement savings plans.

Once you understand the two main building blocks of a sound financial plan and the need to constantly focus on both, you will have taken an important first step toward achieving financial security. The more complicated task is figuring out which products will work best for you and when is the appropriate time to acquire those products.

Why are you investing?

One important task in developing your financial plan is to determine why you are investing. To help you think about your investment decisions, here is a list of possible reasons you make particular investments. Place a check mark next to all of the reasons you make investment decisions:

- [ ] To accelerate the growth of your savings
- [ ] To put your available money to work
- [ ] To accumulate a down payment for a home
- [ ] To increase your current purchasing power
- [ ] To decrease your reliance on consumer loans
- [ ] To decrease income lost on interest payments
- [ ] To provide for your children's education
- [ ] To create a sizable retirement nest egg
- [ ] To enable an earlier than expected retirement
- [ ] To increase your wealth, security, and independence
- [ ] To provide advantages for your loved ones and heirs

Where to invest?

The next step is determining where to invest that will accomplish your reasons for investing and will allow you to meet all of your goals. The website www. FinancialSafari.com provides a wealth of information about some of the core insurance products that make up the foundation of the pyramid: life, health, disability and long-term care insurance. Give careful consideration to these products because a financial plan without insurance is really just a savings and investment program that will die or become disabled when you do.

For information regarding the top of the pyramid, and how to meet your savings and investment objectives, there is no shortage of information at newsstands, on television, or on the Internet. The challenge is figuring out how to sort through it all.

Now, compare the pyramid to your own portfolio of investments by listing your investments below:

_____

_____

_____

_____

_____

_____

Do your investments fit into the pyramid?

_____

_____

Do you have an appropriate amount of investments in the foundation of your pyramid? In other words, are your top-of-the-pyramid investments within the maximum amount that you earlier determined should be at risk?

_____

_____

Do your investments fit within your reasons for investing?

_____

_____

Do your investments meet your risk tolerance?

_____

_____

By answering these questions, you are well on your way to developing a sound and complete financial plan. Now, just make sure to take whatever additional steps are needed in order to complete that plan.

TIME VALUE OF MONEY AND THE COST OF WAITING

Procrastinating is one of the biggest mistakes people make with their money. Postponing investment decisions can mean losing money! When you make an investment, you are setting aside money for future income, benefit or profit to meet your financial goals. This means you are letting money work for you instead of working for money.

Today, there are a variety of investment choices. This section discusses the financial benefits of investing, explains some basic investment terms, and hopefully motivates you to start an investment program, if you have not done so already.

Many couples think they do not have enough money to invest. If this is you, consider what happens if you wait to start an investment program.

Example:

Should you start a savings program now with $50 each month or wait 10 years and save $150 each month? You might initially think you should wait 10 years because you expect to earn more income in 10 years. However, look at what happens:

Example		
Saving Now vs. Saving Later Earning 9% Interest		
Beginning	**Monthly Amount Saved**	**End Result 20 Years From Now**
Now	$50	$33,394
In 10 Years	$150	$29,027

The chart above compares the two options over a 20-year period. While the end results do not appear to be substantially different at first glance, consider these "hidden" figures. If you begin investing now, in 20 years you will have invested a total of $12,000; but if you wait 10 years, you'll end up investing a total of $18,000. Thus, if you wait, you will have to

set aside **$6,000 more to earn $4,367 less in 20 years**. Keep in mind, this example assumes you can earn an average of 9% during the 20-year period.

Rule of 72

Something else to consider is the "Rule of 72." This is a quick and simple way to estimate how your money can grow. You can use this rule in two ways.

(1) Divide 72 by the interest rate you expect to earn. This will show how many years it will take to double your money.

Example
Assume you are going to earn 6% interest on your money.
72 / 6% Interest = 12 Years

(2) Divide 72 by the number of years in which you want your money to double. The result is an estimate of the interest rate you will need to earn.

Example
Assume you want your money to double in 6 years.
72 / 6 years = 12% Interest

Now you try the Rule of 72.

What is your current interest rate? _____%

What interest rate would you like to compare to your current interest rate? _____%

Use both interest rates in the formulas below to determine how long it will take you to double your money at your current rate and at your desired rate.

Current Rate:

$$\frac{72}{\underline{\qquad}\%} = \underline{\qquad} \text{Years}$$

Desired Rate

$$\frac{72}{\underline{\qquad}\%} = \underline{\qquad} \text{Years}$$

When to Start Investing

You have now seen how waiting can affect the amount of your savings, and how the Rule of 72 provides information about your interest rate and the time for your money to double; the next step is to decide when to start investing. Below is a list of factors that will allow you to determine when you should start investing:

1) Your income exceeds your spending.
2) You have an emergency savings fund equal to 3 to 6 months' living expenses.
3) All insurance needs, including life, health, disability, and property are covered.

If you begin saving for your retirement early in your life, you will have to put aside much less money each month. If you wait until you are nearing retirement, the amount you will need to save each month could be near impossible. The illustration below shows you how time really is money.

Top 10 Ways To Prepare For Retirement

1. Know your retirement needs.

Retirement is expensive. Experts estimate that you will need about 70 percent of your pre-retirement income – lower earners, 90 percent or more – to maintain your standard of living when you stop working. So, it is important to understand your financial future.

2. Find out about your Social Security benefits.

Currently, Social Security pays the average retiree about 40 percent of pre-retirement earnings. If you contribute to Social Security, you will receive a personal statement each year. If you would like an estimate of your retirement benefits, call the Social Security Administration at 1-800-772-1213 to request a copy.

3. Learn about your employer's pension or profit sharing plan.

If your employer offers a plan, check to see what your benefit is worth. Most employers will provide an individual benefit statement if you request one. Before you change jobs, find out what will happen to your pension. Learn what benefits you may have from previous employment. Find out if you will be entitled to benefits from your spouse's plan. The U.S. Department of Labor, Employee Benefits Security Administration, has several publications that discuss worker's pension benefits. Visit their web site at **www.dol.gov/ebsa**

4. Contribute to a tax-sheltered savings plan.

If your employer offers a tax-sheltered savings plan, such as a 401(k), sign up and contribute all you can. Your taxes will be lower, your company may kick in more, and automatic deductions make it easy. Over time, deferral of taxes and compounding of interest make a big difference in the amount of money you will accumulate.

5. Ask your employer to start a plan.

If your employer does not offer a retirement plan, suggest that it start one. Certain employers can set up simplified plans. For information on simplified employee pensions, order Internal

Revenue Service Publication 590 by calling 1-800-829-3676 or find it online at **www.irs.gov/ formspubs**

6. Put money into an Individual Retirement Account.

You can put up to $4,000 a year ($4,500 if you are 50 or older) into an Individual Retirement Account (IRA) and delay paying taxes on investment earnings until retirement age. If you do not have a retirement plan (or are in a plan and earn less than a certain amount), you can also take a tax deduction for your IRA contributions. Certain restriction apply. IRS Publication 590 contains information about IRAs. You can view or print a copy online at **www.irs.gov/ formspubs**

7. Do not touch your savings.

Do not dip into your retirement savings. You will lose principal and interest, and you may lose tax benefits. If you change jobs, roll over your savings directly into an IRA or your new employer's retirement plan.

8. Start now, set goals, and stick to them.

Start early. As noted previously, the sooner you start saving, the more time your money has to grow. Put time on your side. Make retirement saving a high priority. Then, devise a plan, stick to it, and set goals for yourself. Remember, it is never too late to start; so, start saving now, whatever your age.

9. Consider basic investment principles.

How you save can be as important as how much you save. Inflation and the type of investments you make play important roles in how much you will have saved at retirement. Know how your pension or savings plan is invested because financial security and knowledge go hand in hand.

10. Ask questions.

These tips should point you in the right direction, but you will need more information. Talk to your employer, your bank, your union, or a financial advisor. Ask questions and make sure the answers make sense to you. It is important to get practical advice and to act now.

ANNUITIES

Life spans in the United States have been increasing for over a hundred years. It is now common for people who reach retirement age to live 20 years or more in retirement, most of those years in good health. It is good to live a long and full life, but you want to be sure that your income lasts as long as you do, and its purchasing power is as strong as you are.

How can you manage the risk of "outliving your assets"?

Annuities are a unique financial product that, along with Social Security, employer pensions, your 401(k) plan, IRA and other assets, can enhance your retirement security.

What is an annuity?

An annuity is simply a contract offered by an insurance company. They were initially designed to provide payments to the holder usually after retirement, with the payments being paid out in specified intervals.

All annuities grow tax-deferred, which means that the earnings inside the annuity are not taxed until the money is taken out. An annuity has a death benefit equivalent to the larger of the current value of the annuity or the amount the buyer has paid into it. This death benefit is usually subject to estate and income tax to the heirs.

What are the different types of annuities?

Fixed Annuities

In a *fixed* annuity, there is a "fixed" rate of return. Thus, the insurance company guarantees the principal and a minimum rate of interest so that the money you have in a fixed annuity will grow and will not drop in value.

The growth of the annuity's value and/or the benefits paid may be fixed at a dollar amount or by an interest rate, or they may grow by a specified formula. The growth of the annuity's value and/or the benefits paid does not depend directly or entirely on the performance of the investments the insurance company makes to support the annuity. Fixed annuities are regulated by state insurance departments.

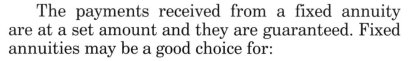

The payments received from a fixed annuity are at a set amount and they are guaranteed. Fixed annuities may be a good choice for:

- conservative investors who value safety and stability.
- those nearing retirement who want to shelter their assets from the volatility of the stock or bond markets.

Variable Annuities

Money in a *variable* annuity is invested in a fund, like a mutual fund, but the fund is only open to investors in the insurance company's variable life insurance and variable annuities. The fund has a particular investment objective. As a result, Stock Market performance determines the annuity's value and the return the investor receives from the money invested.

Most variable annuities are structured to offer investors a variety of securities options including stock and bond funds. The amount of risk the investor is willing to assume should influence the kind of funds selected.

Because there is risk associated with variable annuities, they are regulated by state insurance departments *and* the federal Securities and Exchange Commission. In addition, because of the inherent risk involved in variable annuities, investors should carefully read the entire prospectus before investing in a variable annuity.

Fixed Equity-Indexed Annuities

A fixed *equity-indexed* annuity (also known as an EIA) is a type of fixed annuity, but it is actually a hybrid. It provides a minimum rate of interest, just as a fixed annuity does, but its value is also based on the performance of a specified stock index—usually computed as a fraction of that index's total return.

These EIAs enable people to share in the upside of the Stock Market with absolutely no downside risk. Thus, if the Stock Market goes up, then the investor receives some of that gain; on the other side, however, if the Stock Market goes down, the investor loses nothing because the principal is guaranteed. Only the market gains, and never market losses, are realized. One of the major psychological advantages of an EIA over any other investment that involves risk is that it removes the enormous pressure to sell a stock or equity position that is declining when it really should be held for the long-term. The pressure is removed and life is fun again.

Market-Value-Adjusted Annuities

A *market-value-adjusted* annuity is one that combines two desirable features—the ability to select and fix the time period and interest rate over which your annuity will grow, and the flexibility to withdraw money from the annuity before the end of the time period selected. This withdrawal flexibility is achieved by adjusting the annuity's value, up or down, to reflect the change in the interest rate "market" from the start of the selected time period to the time of withdrawal.

What are the different categories of annuities?

Within the different types of annuities noted above, there are also different categories of annuities. Annuities are often classified by:

- ✎ Nature of the underlying investment – *fixed* or *variable*
- ✎ Primary purpose of accumulation or pay-out – *deferred* or *immediate*
- ✎ Nature of pay-out commitment – *fixed period, fixed amount,* or *lifetime*
- ✎ Tax status – *qualified* or *nonqualified*

Keep in mind, however, that an annuity can be classified in one or more of these categories at the same time.

Immediate Annuities

An *immediate* annuity is designed to begin paying out one time-period after the immediate annuity is purchased. The frequency of the payments depends on how the annuity is structured and the agreement between the parties. For example, if the income is monthly, the first payment comes one month after the immediate annuity is bought.

Split Annuity

A Split Annuity is the combination of a Single Premium Immediate Annuity and a Single Premium Tax-deferred Annuity. The result is an immediate source of income for a guaranteed period of time, and it restores your original principal at the end of that time period. This is possible because a Single Premium Annuity is used to restore the original principal at the end of the guaranteed period. The Single Premium Immediate Annuity provides a guaranteed monthly income for the same time period.

A Split Annuity is advantageous because it allows the investor to start the investment process over at a later date at the then prevailing interest rates. Another advantage of a Split Annuity is that the funds placed in the Single Premium Deferred Annuity policy are available for emergencies with some limitations.

There are some limitations for Split Annuities based on the issue age of the policy or on the use of Split Annuities. For example, non-qualified funds are available for individuals age 0-85, while qualified funds are available for individuals age 0-70. The immediate income periods for Split Annuities range from 3-20 years. If an individual withdraws from an Annuity prior to age 59½, the IRS may impose a 10% penalty tax.

Split annuities, as with other annuities, are guaranteed by state law in accordance with the chart referenced previously.

Fixed Period vs. Lifetime Annuities

A *fixed period* annuity pays an income for a specified period of time, such as ten years. The amount that is paid does not depend on the age (or continued life) of the person who buys the annuity; rather, the payments depend on the amount paid into the annuity, the length of the payout period, and (if it is a fixed annuity) an interest rate that the insurance company believes it can support for the length of the pay-out period.

A *lifetime* annuity provides income for the remaining life of a person (called the "annuitant"). A variation of lifetime annuities continues the income stream until the second one of two annuitants dies. No other type of financial product promises to do this. The amount of the payments depends on the age of the annuitant (or ages, if it is a two-life annuity), the amount paid into the annuity, and (if it is a fixed annuity) an interest rate that the insurance company believes it can support for the length of the expected pay-out period.

With a "pure" lifetime annuity, the payments stop when the annuitant dies, even if the death occurs a very short time after the payments began. Because many annuity buyers are uncomfortable with this possibility, the insurance companies often will add a guaranteed period—essentially a fixed period annuity—to the lifetime annuity. With this combination, if a person dies before the fixed period ends, the income continues to the person's beneficiaries until the end of that period.

Qualified vs. Non-Qualified Annuities

A *qualified* annuity is one used to invest and disburse money in a tax-favored retirement plan, such as an IRA or Keogh plan or plans governed by Internal Revenue Code sections, 401(k), 403(b), or 457. Under the terms of the plan, money paid into the annuity (called "premiums" or "contributions") is not included in taxable income for the year in which it is paid in. All other tax provisions that apply to non-qualified annuities also apply to qualified annuities.

A *nonqualified* annuity is one purchased separately from, or "outside of," a tax-favored retirement plan. Investment earnings of all annuities, qualified and non-qualified, are tax-deferred until they are withdrawn; at that point they are treated as taxable income (regardless of whether they came from selling capital at a gain or from dividends).

Single Premium vs. Flexible Premium Annuities

A *single premium* annuity is an annuity funded by a single payment. The payment might be invested for growth for a long period of time—a single premium deferred annuity—or invested for a short time, after which payout begins—a single premium immediate annuity. Single premium annuities are often funded by rollovers from other investment vehicles or from the sale of an appreciated asset.

A *flexible premium* annuity is an annuity that is intended to be funded by a series of payments. Flexible premium annuities are only deferred annuities because they are designed to have a significant period of payments into the annuity plus investment growth before any money is withdrawn from them.

Why should I consider purchasing an annuity?

People consider purchasing annuities for a variety of reasons. If you or someone you know is in a phase of life where you are interested in saving money, a deferred annuity can:

> Help you meet your retirement income goals.

Employer-sponsored plans such as a 401(k), 403(b), or Keogh are important parts of a retirement plan. However, because contributions to these plans and to IRAs are limited, they might not provide you with the amount of retirement income that you will need, especially if you started saving for retirement late or had contributions interrupted—perhaps due to job changes and/or family responsibilities. In addition, your Social Security benefits and defined-benefit pension (if you have one) may provide less than you need to retire. You need to keep in mind that the purchasing power of defined-benefit pension income is eroded by inflation.

≈ Help you diversify your investment portfolio.

Investment experts routinely advise that, to get the best return for a given level of risk, people need to diversify their investments. Fixed annuities, in particular, offer a unique asset class because it is an investment that is guaranteed not to decrease and that will actually increase at a specified interest rate (and sometimes even more).

≈ Help you manage your investment portfolio.

When your investments in the various asset classes go beyond the percentage allocations you chose, you can "rebalance" those assets. This can be accomplished by shifting funds from the classes that have grown faster to the ones that have grown more slowly. Doing this with mutual funds may cause you to incur capital gains taxes. However, if you use an annuity, such as a fixed equity indexed annuity, you do not pay capital gains taxes. When you eventually withdraw money from the annuity (which could be many years after the rebalancing), you pay tax at that time at the ordinary income rate.

On the other hand, if you or someone you know is in an phase in life where you need income, an immediate annuity could be the right vehicle for you. An immediate annuity can:

🔺 Help protect you against outliving your assets.

Generally, under the current regime and if the person meets all of the program requirements, Social Security will pay a person retirement income for as long as they live. Likewise, defined-benefit pension plans also pay retirement income for life. However, the only other private investment available that provides an indefinite source of income is an immediate annuity.

🔺 Help protect your assets from creditors.

The most that creditors can generally access is the payments from an immediate annuity as they are made, as opposed to being able to seize the entire investment that can occur with other types of investments. The reason is because the money you gave to the insurance company, in exchange for the payout plan contained in your contract, actually belongs to the company. In addition, some state statutes and court decisions may further protect some or all of the payments from annuities from creditors.

How much should I invest in an annuity?

Unlike a 401(k) or an IRA, there are no limits on the amount that you can invest in an annuity. Whether you are considering a deferred or immediate annuity, the amount of money you should consider putting into an annuity depends on:

- ⏴ Your immediate actual and potential financial needs.
- ⏴ Your long-term financial goals.
- ⏴ Your current savings/investment portfolio.
- ⏴ The range of alternatives available to you.

The most important factor in the list above is your immediate actual and potential financial needs. If you buy a deferred annuity but then have a sudden need for cash, you can usually withdraw a small amount without penalty. However, you will likely pay a penalty if you make a large withdrawal within a few years after purchasing such a deferred annuity.

On the other hand, if you purchase an immediate annuity, you usually cannot get any more than the regular payments. Nevertheless, these immediate annuities can still be a valuable asset if you have other sources of immediate cash that are sufficient for any emergency or unforeseen needs.

Thus, when making the decision of how much to invest in an annuity, you should look at your complete financial situation to ensure that you have adequate funds and available cash to meet your immediate needs, but also have sufficient assets to provide for your long-term existence.

Common Misconceptions

Liquidity

Brokers and other investment advisors who do not offer fixed Equity Index Annuities often try to dissuade investors from purchasing EIAs by saying they are "illiquid." They will usually point to surrender fees and maturity dates.

To clarify this issue, however, you should know that surrender fees are an important aspect of annuities. All annuities have their own set of surrender periods. Surrender charges are necessary because if the annuitant does not stay the course, the insurance company might be forced to sell an investment earlier than it had planned in order to make the money available earlier, which could mean liquidating at a loss. Thus, so the insurance company can guarantee the interest rate it promised, it has to set certain limits regarding withdrawals.

A fair time period is 10 years or less, but this does not have to mean that your money is locked away and untouchable. No two annuities are the same, and as with most things there are some good ones and some bad ones; however, most annuities offer the annuitant the opportunity to take out 5-10% of the annuity value each year *surrender fee free.*

In addition, many annuities also offer an option to borrow up to 50% of the value of the annuity. This can provide annuitants with a substantial sum of funds should some need arise that was not planned. Advantages of borrowing from yourself is that the money, as long as it is paid back, is not treated as income and, thus, not reportable on your income tax return.

Despite what you may hear from brokers, an investment that allows withdrawal of 5-10% of the annuity value deposited each year, and also offers the possibility of borrowing up to 50% of the value, is not an illiquid asset.

The other point brokers often make about annuities is that they have to be held to the maturity date, which is sometimes 30 years away. However, nothing could be further from the truth.

An annuity's maturity date is simply a date in the future at which, if the investor is still holding the annuity at that time, the annuity matures and the entire lump sum is payable to the investor. This is a protection for the investor, despite how it is described by brokers. Although the maturity date is in the future, investors can get a lump sum payment at the end of the surrender period, which usually is 7-  10 years. There is no requirement that the annuity be held until the maturity date. Thus, at any time between the time when the surrender period ends until the annuity matures, the investor can take out all the money they deposited plus all the interest they have earned.

Guarantees

Often times bankers will say that annuities are not FDIC insured, attempting to indicate that they are not as safe as a bank's investments, such as CDs. What these bankers forget to mention is that annuities are protected in a different way, and sometimes to a greater extent, than investments in a bank.

People investing in annuities are actually protected by each state's laws. Each state has a Guaranty Association that guarantees the funds invested with insurance companies in the event that an insurance company has financial difficulties. This is possible because insurance companies are required to put money into a trust account any time an investment is purchased. The amount of protection varies by state, but in many cases the investments with insurance companies are more protected that the investments that are FDIC insured at the bank.

At the end of this chapter is a chart showing the protection provided for annuity investments by state, along with the phone numbers for the various state Guaranty Associations.

Fees and Commissions

Another common thing brokers and bankers try to point to in order to dissuade people from investing in annuities is the fees and commissions. However, with the exception of variable annuities, which are more akin to mutual funds and are often offered by bankers and brokers, there are no out-of-pocket fees and commissions associated with most fixed and indexed annuities.

What bankers and brokers do not mention is that variable annuities and mutual funds are loaded with fees and risk. As a result, your account can be eroded away by market losses, as well as yearly fees and commissions that come out of your account. Not to mention that even when you have a loss for the year, the fees still come out and the broker or banker still gets his or her commission. So they get paid for losing your money!

On the other hand, remember that the beauty of Fixed and Index Annuities is the fact that there is no risk of losing your investment. As a result,

there are no front-end fees — every penny you put into your annuity stays in your annuity. Likewise, no fees or commissions come out of your balances. The agents who offer Fixed and Index annuities are compensated by the insurance companies they recommend and no money is ever taken out of your account unless you take it out yourself.

Here's how Fixed and Index annuity agents get paid: Have you ever used a travel agent? If so, you know that when you use the travel agent you get worry-free trip planning and a greater choice of alternatives. The travel agent has a vast knowledge of the industry and, as a result, can often put together a complete vacation for a lot less then you would ever have dreamed. In addition, you probably remember that using the travel agent did not cost you one penny more and, in many cases, probably saved you money because of the vast array of choices the travel agent had to offer.

Just like a travel agent, Fixed and Index annuity agents charge no fees to their clients. Rather, they are paid a sort of finders fee from the insurance companies they recommend to their clients. Even though it does not cost you a penny, you should still be careful to only work with agents and planners who deal with the strongest companies (A.M. Best ranked grade A and higher).

Because there are no fees or commissions paid to the Fixed or Index annuity agent, 100% of what you put into your annuity stays in your annuity. As a result, you can feel confident knowing *your* best interests are being taken into consideration. Investing in annuities ensures that not one penny of fees or commissions ever come out of your investment so every penny goes to work for you, not into a broker's or banker's pocket.

Clearing the Confusion

Brokers and bankers will also try to convince you that mutual funds and stocks are across-the-board a better investment than annuities. However, this is simply not the case. While they may be appropriate in some stages of life, they are not the best investment choice when you are at a stage in life where you need to secure your earnings for a worry-free retirement.

We have learned that approximately 95 million Americans have invested $7.6 trillion of their life savings in mutual funds. Are they all investment gurus or is this similar to what we see on the news each year when hundred's of whales beach themselves simply because they are all following each other in what is often referred to as the "Herd Mentality"? How can so many be wrong?

The mutual fund business stands on the following premise: "Professional money managers can beat the market." However, based on performance records, this premise is absolutely false. In fact, "professional money manager" seems to be is an oxymoron when applied to mutual funds. This is because the record shows mutual funds have under-performed the stock market, and the S&P 500 index has beaten most actively managed mutual funds each year. Sadly, just one mutual fund manager in four even matches the performance of the overall market. This dismal record is a function of many factors, but conflicts of interest, fraud, high fees, and overtrading are high on the list. Mutual funds are the only investment where the investor pays a fee to get in, an on-going management fee while owning them, and then a separation or redemption fee when sold. Even with "no loads," investors still pay fees.

How is that fair when the market value of a mutual fund can drop but the investor may still owe taxes? The feverish portfolio turnover rate has transformed mutual fund investing from "long term" to "short term."

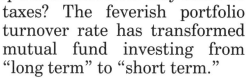

Thus, before you consider investing in mutual funds, you should be aware that portfolio pumping, market timing, window dressing, closet indexing, front running, and putting portfolios on "show" creates an image of success to mask poor performance. Not only are these terms foreign to investors, they are also a mystery to the average broker. In fact, it seems that most mutual fund investors have no idea what they are buying, and neither do the brokers who are selling the funds.

Unfortunately, financial advisors are, like their clients, often unaware of "insider practices" and "marketing spin" and actually believe their clients are getting diversification, safety, and money managers that beat the market. However, many mutual fund companies have admitted defrauding investors. The list includes some of the biggest names in the business and it continues to grow. These companies have been charged with enriching themselves by skimming away the profits of "ordinary investors" and sharing it with their institutional clients. The hundreds of millions paid to settle claims, and the jail time given to dishonest managers, have not made the "average investor" whole again. Corruption, poor performance and conflicts of interest are not the exception, it seems to be the rule.

It also seems that mutual funds have evolved from being "about investment" to "about marketing." The billions of advertising dollars spent each year on marketing spin counteracts the dismal performance and fraudulent activity. And who do you think pays for these advertisements??? You do, with the fees these companies charge each year. It is quite ironic that ordinary investors end up financing their own deception. Mutual funds have seemingly turned into a losing game for many investors.

Mutual fund investing is like driving in rush hour: stressfully switching lanes to get ahead with an increased risk of disaster. Investing in annuities, on the other hand, means staying in the same lane with no stress and always a positive return.

Why select mutual funds that consistently under-perform the market, create current tax liabilities and impose high fees when there are infinitely better choices? As noted above, Fixed and Index Annuities, for example, offer substantial tax advantages, are guaranteed to never have a market loss, and provide risk free participation in the stock and bond markets. Plus, there are no front-end charges, no on-going fees, and exit penalties only when an investor gets out early. Smart investing in vehicles such as annuities helps investors pay less in taxes and fees, which leaves more money to work for the investor.

One thing to be aware of is that if you have a variable annuity, instead of a Fixed or Indexed Annuity, you are not protected from fees and commissions, not to mention market risk. In fact, your fees can be even worse then actually holding the individual mutual funds. Variable annuity sales people are great at hyping the potential returns and sometimes fail to mention the fees and risk of loss of principal due to commissions and market risk exposure.

As a result, if you have variable annuities, you must read the prospectus. Any investment that involves risk, fees, or commissions must include a prospectus. You should not just skim that prospectus; rather, you need to read it from front to back, and then read it again to make sure you completely understand that investment and all of the risk, fees, and commissions included.

Do not let yourself be pressured by your banker, broker, or a sales person into signing something unless you are 100% certain you understand this investment. In addition, you should be careful of whom you are talking to regarding your investments. Many times you may discover the "Financial Advisor" you think you have is nothing more than a stockbroker or mutual fund peddler.

Here's the bottom line regarding your best investment choices: It is not fair that when you have a good year in the market, you must share your gains with your broker but when you have a down year in the market based on the broker's advice, not only do they not share in your loss, but many times they still take their commissions and fees out of your dwindling balance, depleting it even more.

These misconceptions show why you need to do your homework when making investment decisions. You should not be fooled by misinformed advisors who may want to lead you away from secure investments with no risk into risky investments just so they can make a commission. Make sure you know and trust your financial advisors, and also understand the nature of every investment recommended. Be sure that your investment goals are considered and never do anything unless you are completely comfortable and knowledgeable of your investment decision. The following chart is for fixed annuities.

Financial Safari — Be Prepared, Not Surprised

State	Max. liability for present value of an annuity contract	State Guaranty Association Phone Numbers
Alabama	$100,000	(205) 879-2202
Alaska	$100,000	(907) 243-2311
Arizona	$100,000	(602) 364-3863
Arkansas	$300,000	(501) 371-2776
California	80% not to exceed $100,000	(323) 782-0182
Colorado	$100,000	(303) 292-5022
Connecticut	$100,000	(860) 529-3495
Delaware	$100,000	(302) 456-3656
Dist. of Col.	$300,000	(202) 434-8771
Florida	$100,000	(904) 398-3644
Georgia	$100,000	(770) 621-9835
Hawaii	$100,000	(808) 528-5400
Idaho	$100,000	(208) 378-9510
Illinois	$100,000	(773) 714-8050
Indiana	$100,000	(317) 636-8204
Iowa	$100,000	(515) 283-3163
Kansas	$100,000	(785) 271-1199
Kentucky	$100,000	(502) 895-5915

State	Max. liability for present value of an annuity contract	State Guaranty Association Phone Numbers
Louisiana	$100,000	(225) 381-0656
Maine	$100,000	(207) 633-1090
Maryland	$100,000	(410) 998-3907
Massachusetts	$100,000	(413) 744-8483
Michigan	$100,000	(517) 372-3863
Minnesota	$100,000	(651) 407-3149
Mississippi	$100,000	(601) 981-0755
Missouri	$100,000	(573) 634-8455
Montana	$100,000	(262) 965-5761
Nebraska	$100,000	(402) 474-6900
Nevada	$100,000	(775) 329-8387
New Hampshire	$100,000	(603) 226-9114
New Jersey	$100,000	(973) 623-3989
New Mexico	$100,000	(505) 237-9397
New York	$500,000	(212) 909-6813
No. Carolina	$300,000	(919) 833-6838
North Dakota	$100,000	(701) 235-4108
Ohio	$100,000	(614) 442-6601
Oklahoma	$300,000	(405) 272-9221
Oregon	$100,000	(503) 588-1974

State	Max. liability for present value of an annuity contract	State Guaranty Association Phone Numbers
Pennsylvania	$100,000	(610) 975-0572
Puerto Rico	$100,000	(787) 765-2095
Rhode Island	$100,000	(401) 273-2921
South Carolina	$300,000	(803) 536-9874
South Dakota	$100,000	(605) 336-0177
Tennessee	$100,000	(615) 242-8758
Texas	$100,000	(512) 476-5101
Utah	$200,000	(801) 572-1218
Vermont	$100,000	(802) 244-8540
Virginia	$100,000	(804) 282-2240
Washington	$500,000	(425) 562-3128
West Virginia	$100,000	(304) 733-6904
Wisconsin	$300,000	(608) 242-9473
Wyoming	$100,000	(303) 292-5022

Disclaimer:

Mr. D'Arruda and FinancialSafari.com are not to be held responsible for the accuracy of this information. You are advised to call your state insurance department prior to purchasing any annuity contract.

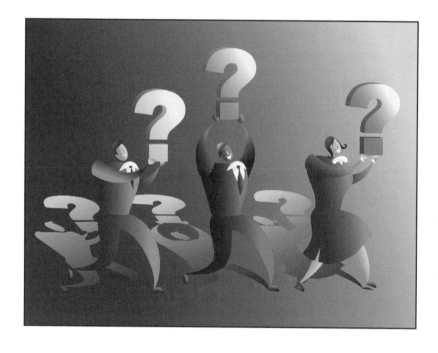

RETIREMENT STRATEGIES

The following represent a few common retirement strategies:

- 1035 Exchange
- RMD Management
- Social Security Tax Avoidance
- Split Annuity
- Stretch IRA

> ## It's Not What You Earn;
> ## It's What You Get to Keep That Counts!

We will discuss each of these strategies in more detail below.

1035 Exchange

Congratulations, you have a new job – retirement! Now you must decide what to do with the assets you have accumulated in your retirement plan.

One option is to leave the money where it is, if this is allowed by your former employer. Even if it is allowed, however, this may not be the best decision.

You may have greater investment options and greater flexibility in withdrawing your funds if you roll over your assets into your own IRA. Whether you decide to move your money for more options and flexibility, or simply because the current investment is not performing adequately, moving your money to your own IRA can be accomplished using a 1035 Exchange as allowed by the Tax Code. As noted above, if you chose to roll your money into an annuity, you would be using Section 1035 to reconfigure your assets in order to gain guaranteed growth and at the same time get rid of some uncertainty.

You can also choose to convert your assets into cash. However, this is often the least desirable option because if your former employer sends you a check they are required to withhold 20% for federal taxes. In addition, if you do not deposit the balance in another retirement plan or IRA within 60 days, the entire amount becomes taxable. In addition, if you are under the age of 59½ you may be subject to an additional 10% penalty.

RMD Management

Once you retire, you can postpone withdrawing money from your retirement plan until you have reached the age of 70½. By April 1st of the year after you turn 70½, you must take your first required minimum distribution (RMD). Thereafter, you must take annual distributions.

The amount you are required to take out is usually figured out by the company holding the account based on specialized mortality tables that the IRS publishes. It is important to make the required distribution by the end of the calendar year in order to avoid a 50% penalty of the amount of the distribution. Ordinary income taxes are also due on the entire amount if you do not take the required distribution.

To calculate the year's RMD amount, take the age of the retiree and find the corresponding distribution period on the chart below. Then divide the value of the IRA by the distribution period to find the RMD.

The chart on the next page shows the distribution period for investments in the name of an individual. There is a different chart for investments that are jointly owned. The IRS provides these life expectancy tables. Table I (for individual life expectancy) and Table II (for joint life expectancy) can be found in IRS Publication 939.

Age of Retiree	Distribution Period (years)	Age of Retiree	Distribution Period (years)	Age of Retiree	Distribution Period (years)
70	27.4	86	14.1	102	5.5
71	26.5	87	13.4	103	5.2
72	25.6	88	12.7	104	4.9
73	24.7	89	12	105	4.5
74	23.8	90	11.4	106	4.2
75	22.9	91	10.8	107	3.9
76	22	92	10.2	108	3.7
77	21.2	93	9.6	109	3.4
78	20.3	94	9.1	110	3.1
79	19.5	95	8.6	111	2.9
80	18.7	96	8.1	112	2.6
81	17.9	97	7.6	113	2.4
82	17.1	98	7.1	114	2.1
83	16.3	99	6.7	115 or older	1.9
84	15.5	100	6.3		
85	14.8	101	5.9		

The value used to calculate the RMD is based on the total value of each plan as of December 31st of the preceding year. When calculating the distribution for the second year, it is reduced by any distribution made in that year to satisfy the RMD for the first year.

The age 70½ RMD requirement applies to people who have an IRA, 401(k), SEP-IRA, TSA, or SIMPLE Plan. Roth IRA's are *not* covered by this RMD rule. If you have more than one retirement plan that requires a minimum distribution, a separate calculation is required for each plan. However, once the RMD amount is determined from the combination of plans, it can be taken from one plan.

Example:

Peter was born on June 11, 1928. He turned 70½ in 1999. When do you think Peter must begin taking his RMD?

Answer: April 1, 2000

Now, assume that Peter's IRA account balance as of December 31, 1998, is $49,000. Based on Peter's age, what is his distribution period (or life expectancy), using the chart earlier?

Answer: 26.5 year

So, what is Peter's RMD?

Answer: $49,000 / 26.5 yrs = $1,849

Thus, $1,849.06 must be distributed to Peter by April 1, 2000.

Now, let's assume that this is a joint account and Peter's wife, the primary beneficiary, turned 60 in September 1999.

Based on their ages on December 31, 1999, the joint life expectancy for Peter, age 71, and Peter's wife, age 60, is 23.4 years (from IRS Table II). What is Peter's RMD?

Answer: $49,000 / 23.4 yrs = $2,094

Thus, the RMD for Peter's first distribution year is $2,094. This amount must be distributed to Peter by April 1, 2000.

After the first distribution, you may choose one of two ways to calculate your RMD. The first alternative is to refigure your or your spouse's life expectancy each year. Another option is to reduce the life expectancy by one year for each year that has elapsed since you initially determined your life expectancy. This method is known as term certain.

Stretch, or Multi-Generational, IRA

Congress created the Individual Retirement Account (IRA) to provide a tax incentive for individuals to save for retirement. It has proven to be one of the most beneficial pieces of legislation ever enacted. The Tax Code allows people to contribute "pre-tax" dollars to an IRA account, resulting in tax savings at the time of the contribution. In addition, earnings accumulate inside the IRA account on a tax-deferred basis, allowing for the accumulation of substantial savings at an accelerated rate. One advantage IRA's offer over "after-tax" investments is that it allows the money that would have been paid in taxes to remain in the account and earn interest for many years; thus, combining the power of compound interest with that of tax-deferral.

In January 2001 the IRS issued new rules governing the distribution of IRAs making it easier for you to plan for retirement while still providing for the income needs of you, your spouse, and your family using your accumulated IRA funds. Normally, distributions from an IRA would begin at a person's retirement (after age 59½), since the purpose of IRAs is to provide income for retirement. However, many people do not have an immediate need for income from their IRA at age 59½ or for some period of time thereafter. As a result, distributions may be postponed until age 70½, the Required Beginning Date (RBD) for IRA distributions. If you can postpone your distributions until the RBD, your account can grow larger, which increases your account value.

The idea behind the Stretch, or Multi-generational, IRA is simple - the longer you are able to "stretch" your IRA distribution, the larger your account grows. One of the best features of the new 2001 Rules is that smaller RMD have been established. Now, an IRA owner can calculate the RMD by using the IRS tables. (See Individual Table earlier.) If you postpone taking any distributions until the RBD and then only withdraw the RMD, you can stretch your IRA benefits over a longer period of time. This reduces your current income tax liability and also increases the long-term benefits to your family.

Stretching your IRA distributions allows you to maximize the power of tax-deferred earnings, which will enable you to create a long-lasting guaranteed stream of income for you and your loved ones over multiple generations. The Stretch IRA can literally turn an account currently worth thousands into millions. The key to transforming your current IRA into a family legacy lies in proper utilization of the Stretch IRA program.

If the IRA owner dies before the spouse, the IRS Rules allow a "Spousal Rollover" of the IRA. Thus, the spouse assumes ownership of the IRA and begins new RMD based on the spouse's age. The Spousal Rollover provides more security and independence for the spouse because it "stretches" IRA income over a longer distribution period, protecting the spouse against running out of income prematurely.

Also in the 2001 IRS Rules, IRA owners can "stretch" IRA distributions over the individual life expectancies of their children and grandchildren. Prior to 2001, most IRAs were structured to force a 5-year distribution to beneficiaries. This created a tax "time bomb" when the IRA

> **"He Who Fails to Plan,**
>
> **Plans to Fail**

owner died. After the 2001 Rules, however, an IRA owner can control the timing of the inherited IRA distributions to children and grandchildren by choosing to base the distributions on the life expectancy of the heir. This allows you to fully maximize the power of tax-deferral because the IRA proceeds left to younger people will grow to surprisingly large amounts over time — stretching thousands of dollars into millions.

Example:

Kay has a grandchild, Carrie, who is 25 years old. Carrie inherits an IRA with a balance of $100,000. If the IRA is not stretched, then Carrie would have a major tax bill and she would actually only inherit less than $80,000. However, if Carrie's distributions are stretched over her lifetime, her distributions can total $1,694,669. This is dramatic increase over the $100,000 IRA and much more than the $80,000 Carrie would have inherited if Kay had not stretched the IRA.

Whether you are making contributions and accumulating wealth in your IRA, or whether you have already started taking distributions, you can still make plans that will allow you take advantage of the Rules that will maximize your IRA account value and will allow you to increase the amount you are able to leave to your family. Your IRA dollars can be used to pay college tuition, help buy that first new home, or serve as start-up capital for a new business venture. Your family will benefit from your loving foresight for years and even generations after you are gone.

Social Security Tax Avoidance

In 1983, Congress passed legislation allowing up to 50% of your Social Security to be taxed when combined income exceeded threshold limits. This ruling came into effect because bureaucrats realized that half of Social Security Income originated from contributions paid by employers. In 1993 the law was amended again to allow up to 85% of Social Security Income to be taxed under certain conditions.

If income (which includes half of Social Security), exceeds certain thresholds, up to 85% of the amount received from Social Security could be subject to tax.

So the next question should be, *"What income is considered threshold income?"*

The following diagram demonstrates investments that could be included as a threshold:

Income Included as Threshold	Yes	No
Deferred Annuity		X
Pension	X	
Income from Mortgages	X	
US Treasuries	X	
Certificates of Deposit	X	
Money Market Accounts	X	
Passbook Savings	X	
Credit Union Savings	X	
Dividends – Stocks	X	
Dividends – Mutual Funds	X	
Capital Gains	X	

As you can see, income from deferred annuities is not included as threshold income. This is the only interest-producing asset that allows interest to grow without being included as threshold income.

One of the many benefits of annuities not being included as threshold income is that taxable interest is replaced with tax-deferred interest. This can help to reduce or eliminate the tax on Social Security!

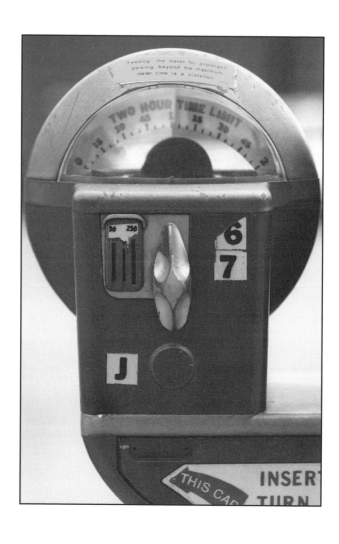

LIFE INSURANCE

Life insurance can play a vital and valuable role at virtually every stage of your life. However, while there are many reasons to buy life insurance, the primary reasons people purchase life insurance are to replace income and to pay for costs associated with a person's death.

The main reason people purchase life insurance is to replace the income you are generating, which someone else relies on, in the event of your death. It is commonly used in one- or two-earner families with young children such that if one earner dies, life insurance will enable the survivors to continue on without having to make financial sacrifices.

Life insurance is also used to pay for one-time costs associated with death: funeral or burial costs, administration costs (i.e., for probate and transferring property to the heirs), estate and inheritance taxes, and outstanding debts (such as final medical expenses not covered by health insurance).

There are many choices to make when buying life insurance: how much to buy, which type to buy, and what company to choose. It is important to work with a knowledgeable professional who understands your needs, answers your questions, and helps you find the best insurance for you. A knowledgeable insurance professional can help you determine how much insurance you need, but this often depends on the amount of income you need to replace should something happen to you, the anticipated costs you wish to cover if the insurance is for that purpose, as well as the actual cost of the insurance. In addition, your insurance professional should also be able to help you select a company that offers an insurance policy best able to meet your needs.

The more difficult question is what type of insurance to buy. Basically, there are two types of life insurance — *Term and Permanent.*

A Term policy is insurance that lasts for a set amount of time, usually referred to as the term. Terms can be found from five (5) years to thirty (30) years, or possibly more. The longer the term, the more the yearly cost. You pay the premiums (costs) during the term and if you die during the term, your beneficiary will receive whatever the death benefit or amount of insurance the policy contained. Once the term is over, you can either renew the policy or choose to let it terminate. However, when a term expires, if you choose to renew the policy, the cost is usually significantly more than the cost during the initial term (sometimes double or triple the cost, or more) because you have aged during that initial term. To the insurance company, you are considered a higher risk because you are older and more likely to die during the renewal term purely based on life expectancy tables. People often compare buying term insurance to renting a house: you do not build any equity and the costs continue to go up if you decide to purchase.

Permanent Insurance, on the other hand, is a policy that stays in effect throughout your lifetime as long as you pay the premiums. You pay the premiums for a set amount of time, sometimes this is for your whole life but there is often a set time after which the amount you have paid reaches a level where the policy is fully paid for so the policy stays in effect for your lifetime but you do not have to pay any further premiums. When you die, your beneficiary will receive the amount of the death benefit. In this type of policy it is also possible to accumulate a cash value account as you pay your premiums. This cash value can be compared to building equity in your home. You can borrow against this cash value, and, if you ever choose to cancel or surrender your policy, the insurance company will pay or refund you this cash value (after any fees or charges are taken out) to you. This is called the cash surrender value. Permanent insurance is great for someone who never wants to worry about a day when they cannot afford to keep their insurance. The two main types of permanent policies are known as Universal Life and Whole Life.

With the major health advances in medicine over the past ten years, and the fact that we as a society are now living longer, many insurance companies have lowered their rates. Thus, it is often possible for someone who purchased a cash value policy years ago to basically exchange that old policy for a new and better policy with more death benefit but without any increase in cost. Some have received double their death benefit just by shopping around and finding a policy that is better now than the policy they purchased years ago. However, you should never cancel your current insurance policy until you are approved and have the newly issued policy in your hands.

Life Insurance Quiz

You might already know some important things about life insurance. To test your knowledge, take this life insurance quiz by answering true or false to the following questions:

_____ 1. I should have life insurance in an amount two times my annual income.

False. The general rule of thumb is that a wage-earner should own life insurance equal to five to eight times his or her gross annual income. However, you should analyze your own specific situation when you decide how much insurance to buy because someone with no children and substantial savings will need less insurance compared to someone of the same age with young children or an aging parent and little in savings.

_____ 2. I am considering financing the purchase of a new car; thus, I should buy credit life insurance to cover the loan in case anything happens to me.

False. In the event of your premature death, if your family would be unable to pay off the car loan, then it will probably be short of financial resources for other things. As a result, you should own some type of life insurance – either permanent or term. However, credit life insurance is usually more expensive than regular term insurance and it is limited since it would only be used to pay off the car loan. If you had a regular term life policy, your family would be able to use the money to meet any

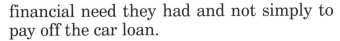

financial need they had and not simply to pay off the car loan.

_____ 3. The cash value and the face value of a permanent life insurance policy are not the same thing.

True. The cash value is the amount available if you surrender a policy early or borrow against it whereas the face value is the money that will be paid at your death or at the maturity of the policy.

_____ 4. Term insurance is always cheaper, so it is a better buy.

False. Term insurance, which pays the face value if you die during the specified term, is cheaper when you are young, but it often costs significantly more if you continue to need it later in life. As a result, it is best to purchase term insurance to cover short-term needs should you die prematurely: paying off a mortgage or putting your children through college. If you are going to consider purchasing term insurance, look into a policy that starts as a term policy but can be converted into a permanent policy at a later date without a medical examination. This will help you make sure you can meet any needs that arise in the future that you are not able to identify at the time you purchase the life insurance.

_____ 5. Permanent insurance provides lifelong protection, so it is always a better choice.

False. Permanent insurance policies accumulate cash value, which can be used in many ways.

However, commissions and administrative costs that are high in the early years make permanent insurance an expensive mistake if you do not keep it in force. Thus, you should only buy permanent insurance if you expect to keep it for many years.

_____ 6. Permanent insurance policies are all different so it is important to understand the individual policy before purchasing it.

True. While all permanent insurance accumulates cash value, there are distinct types of permanent insurance: whole life, universal life, and variable life. Whole life policies offer a fixed face amount on the policy, and the premiums remain level and must be paid on a regular basis. On the other hand, a universal life policy is more flexible in that you can pay premiums at any time, in virtually any amount. In addition, you can change the amount of the death benefit to suit your needs. Variable life policies have varying death benefits and cash values depending on the performance of the underlying portfolio of investments you select. If your investments perform well, you will have a higher death benefit and a higher cash value, but if your investments do not perform well you can expect less. Some variable life policies do guarantee a minimum death benefit.

_____ 7. I have a whole life insurance policy, but I missed a premium payment when I was sick; however, I'm sure my policy wouldn't lapse that quickly so it is still in effect.

True. Most insurance companies generally allow a 30-day or 31-day "grace period." Thus, as long as the missing premium is paid within this time, then the policy will not lapse. However, you should be aware that the insurance company may draw from your cash value in a permanent policy to keep the premium payment up to date if you miss the deadline. If for some reason you cannot make a payment because of a disability, your policy may contain a waiver of the premium payments during your disability. If this is the case, you do not have to make your premium payments during your disability and your life insurance will remain in full force and effect.

_____ 8. If I do not need life insurance any more, I need to give careful consideration to keeping the policy anyway because there are many things the proceeds could be used for.

True. Letting a life insurance policy lapse could be an expensive mistake. You may have other assets to support your family in the event of your death, but the proceeds of your life insurance policy can be used to pay for things such as any estate taxes that may be due. In addition, in the event that you do not want to keep paying premiums, you may be able to use the cash value in a permanent policy to convert the policy to paid-up status.

_____ 9. I have decided that I need a different type of life insurance than I currently have so I am going to let my current policy lapse and buy a new policy.

False. If this is the case, be very careful. You should never drop one policy for another without careful consideration. There are instances in which making this change could make sense, such as where you are still paying premiums on a universal life policy that should have been paid up years ago. However, if you have had the policy for a number of years, meaning that you are older now than when you purchased the current policy, a new policy could be a lot more expensive. In addition, if your health has deteriorated since you bought the current policy, you might find that you cannot get insurance coverage. As a result, you should never give up an old policy before a new one has actually been issued.

In addition, as noted above, if you do have a universal policy that should have been paid up years ago but you are still paying premiums, it may be possible to purchase a new policy offering an increased death benefit for no additional expense. However, because you are older now and your health may have changed, you need to make sure you qualify for any new policy before letting go of the old policy.

LONG TERM CARE INSURANCE

Due to old age, mental or physical illness, or injury, some people find themselves in need of help with eating, bathing, dressing, and other physical activities. Long-term care insurance can help you pay for such care in the future if you end up having such a need.

Long-term care is a misnomer, however, because the situation may not be permanent so it may not last for a long time. Some people who need assistance may only need that assistance for a few months. Many people think that long-term care is provided exclusively in a nursing home. Such care can be provided in nursing homes, but it can also be provided in an adult day care centers, in assisted living facilities, or even at home.

Assistance with activities of daily living, called "custodial care," may be provided in the same place as (and is often confused with) "skilled care." Skilled care means medical, nursing, or rehabilitative services, including helping people take medicine, taking blood pressure or other monitoring, or other similar services. This must be distinguished from custodial care because Medicare and most private health insurance plans will only pay for skilled care and not custodial care.

Will you need long-term care?

This is a question you must answer for yourself. However, current research has shown the following:

⏜ Of a group of healthy 65-year-olds, in their lifetime:

➤ 56% will not ever use a nursing home,

➤ 12% will use a nursing home for less than 3 months,

➤ 9% will use a nursing home for 3 months to a year,

➤ 15% will use a nursing home for 1 year to 5 years, and

➤ 8% will use a nursing home for 5 years or longer.

The problem is you cannot wait until you need long-term care insurance to purchase it. People who wait until they are a little older often find that they no longer qualify for such insurance because of their age and health.

Wakely Consulting Group, an actuarial firm, studied applicants for long-term care insurance in 2003-2004. They found that

⏜ 11% in their 50s were rejected,

⏜ 19% in their 60s were rejected, and

⏜ 43% in their 70s were rejected.

A Milliman actuary estimated that 15% to 25% of people in the over-65 age group are uninsurable for long-term care.

A report from the Henry J. Kaiser Foundation indicated that there are over five million people age 18-64 who need some type of long-term care.

The latest data from the National Center for Health Statistics reported that roughly 160,000 people living in nursing homes were under age 65 (nearly 10 percent of the total). Of those receiving home health care services, roughly 400,000 were under 65 (about 30% of the total).

Should you buy long-term care insurance?

Some questions you need to ask yourself:

- If I am in need of long-term care services and have to pay for them out-of-pocket, what assets do I have that I can use?
- Do I have enough money to pay for four or more years in a nursing home, an assisted living facility, or home health care?

If you are over 65, you should not rely on Medicare or private health insurance. Medicare does not pay for custodial care, and private health insurance rarely pays any of the cost of long-term care.

If you expect to have very little money when you need long-term care services, you might qualify for Medicaid, a government program that pays the medical and long-term care expenses of lower income people. People in this situation, probably should not buy long-term care insurance because their state's Medicaid program should pay for their long-term care expenses.

If you anticipate that you will have significant assets when the need for long-term care services arises, you also probably should not buy long-term care insurance. Instead, you should plan your investing so you can pay for that care as a regular expense at the time you need that care. It has been suggested that if your net worth is in the $2 million range, not including the value of your home, you can safely skip buying long-term care insurance and treat long-term care expenses, if they eventually arise, as you do other bills. Obviously this will depend on your investments and the structure of your portfolio. You should consult a financial advisor to discuss your specific situation.

For people that fall in between these two extremes, owning long-term care insurance, like all other insurance coverage, offers peace-of-mind benefits as well as financial ones. As an example, a recent survey of people age 50 and over asked how confident they were that they could pay for long-term care services if they needed them. Among the people who had long-term care policies, 52% said they were very confident and another 40% said they were somewhat confident. Among people who did not already own a long-term care policy, only 8% were very confident and only 27% were somewhat confident that they could pay for long-term care expenses.

It is often helpful to consult a qualified financial advisor and/or long-term care insurance agent to discuss your current financial situation in order to determine if you need to purchase long-term care insurance.

What is the best age to buy long-term care insurance?

In general, it is a good idea to buy long-term care insurance before you are 60 years old, for two reasons:

1. The younger you are when you apply, the less likely it is that you will be rejected. If you apply in your 50s, there is a one in ten chance you will be rejected. If you apply in your 60s, the chance of rejection is two in ten. If you apply in your 70s, the chance of rejection is four in ten.

2. The younger you are when you apply, the lower the premium will be for a given set of benefits and features. Generally, once the premium is set, it stays the same for the life

of the policy, unless the claims for the group of people who bought that type of policy require that rates for the group be raised.

Should you invest instead of buying long-term care insurance?

Many people under 55 years old think that since the likelihood of long-term care outlays is many years in the future, they can invest the money they would otherwise spend for long-term care insurance premiums in order to earn additional money on that investment. The thinking is that if the need arises in the future for long-term care, then they could just draw on the investment to pay for the services needed, and if no long-term care is ever needed then the money in the investment could be used for other needs, or could be left to heirs or a charity.

This strategy could work if the need for long-term care arises in the distant future such that you would have plenty of time to earn money on your investment. However, this strategy could leave you vulnerable if your need for long-term care services arises when you are in your late 50s, 60s, or early 70s. In addition, this strategy might not work well if you happen to need the long-term care services for a long time, regardless of whether the need did not actually arise until you were 80 years old.

Example:

Jane is 55 years old now and knows she will not need long-term care for 30 years, when she is

85 years old. She is going to start saving $2,000.00 per year now for her long-term care needs in an investment that grows at 5% per year, net after taxes. After 30 years, Jane's savings will have grown to $139,500.00.

Now, assume today's monthly cost of round-the-clock home health care grows, due to inflation, by only 3% per year, from $12,000 per month to $28,300 per month in 30 years.

If all these assumptions prove to be true, Jane's savings would be able to pay for five months of round-the-clock home care or maybe nine months of nursing home care. However, if Jane needed more money – possibly due to the cost of long-term care services growing faster than 3% per year – she would have to liquidate other assets that she had not planned to liquidate, if she had any other assets to liquidate.

(This example does not represent the premium for a long-term care policy for a 55-year-old because premiums vary considerably depending on the daily benefit amount selected, the length of the benefit period, the length of the waiting period, inflation, and other policy features. This example was merely meant to show how savings may or may not adequately provide for long term care needs.)

As noted above, whether or not you need to buy long-term care insurance is a personal decision and one you should discuss with your family and a qualified financial advisor or long-term care insurance agent.

KEEP AN EYE ON SPENDING

Why You Buy What You Buy

Today's marketplace is full of choices. Whether you buy aspirin, a car or truck, it takes time

to sort through the many brands, makes, models or sizes. Making your selections may pose a problem if you are a discriminating customer. Whatever your financial situation, it is a good idea to take a good look at how you spend your income – what is being purchased and why it is being purchased.

Before You Buy

Before you make any purchase, here are some useful suggestions to help you analyze the purchase:

- Use the Rule of 3. Look at three alternatives, such as 3 models, 3 brands, or 3 stores.

- Compare prices. Do not assume an item is a bargain just because it is advertised as one.

⏜ Do not rush into a large purchase because the "price is only good today."

⏜ Ask about the seller's refund or exchange policy.

⏜ Read the unit price labels at the grocery store. Unit pricing allows you to compare the price ounce-for-ounce, pound-for-pound, etc. Keep in mind, larger packages are not always cheaper than smaller sizes.

⏜ Do not rely on a salesperson's promises. Get everything in writing. Deal only with reliable companies.

⏜ Do not sign a contract without reading it first. Make sure there are no blank spaces or parts you do not understand.

After You Buy

Even after you have made a purchase, it is not too late to do your homework about that purchase. Here are some helpful suggestions:

⏜ Read and follow product and service instructions.

⏜ Keep all sales receipts, warranties, service contracts, and instructions.

⏜ If you have a problem, contact the company as soon as possible. Keep a written record of all contacts.

Reasons You Made Certain Purchases

Often times people make major purchases of items that they do not necessarily need or may not even want. To plug these "spending leaks," as we refer to them, you need to analyze why you decided to buy the item or service.

The first step is to list five (5) significant items you have purchased since you have been married.

1. _____

2. _____

3. _____

4. _____

5. _____

After you have listed the purchases, answer each of the questions below.

🔺 Was it bought for a need or want?

🔺 Was it bought for status?

🔺 Was it bought for friendship or love?

🔺 Was it bought for power?

🔺 Was it bought under pressure?

🔺 Was it bought for a collection?

🔺 Was it bought as a reward?

Buying for status, friendship, or love are emotional uses of money. Likewise, controlling or punishing others by withholding money, and overspending to get back at another family member, are also emotional uses of money. While there is nothing to say that purchases made for emotional reasons are bad, it helps to understand why purchases are made when you analyze your future purchases.

Where to Turn for Product Information

Consumers' Research is an independent, nonprofit organization, for the purpose of providing the public with scientific, technical, and educational information. They publish the magazine, *Consumers' Research*, using data believed to be accurate. Consumers' Research is not supported by manufacturers, dealers, or any government agencies. It does not permit any person or firm to make commercial use of its findings, and the publishers and editors do not assume responsibility for any injuries or damages resulting from the use of the products or services described in the magazine.

Consumer's Union is one of the most sought after sources for objective and reliable buying data. This nonprofit organization exists to provide consumers with information and advice on goods, services, health, and personal finance. Many of their findings are reported in their monthly publication – *Consumer Reports*. Consumer's Union accepts no advertising and buys all the products they test on the open market. Because of these practices, it is a good idea to check out *Consumer Reports* before buying big ticket items. It is at least a starting point for a consumer trying to make a buying decision.

Consumer Resource Handbook is updated every two years by the U.S. Office of Consumer Affairs and lists offices you can contact for help with consumer problems or questions. The handbook also provides tips on several consumer issues. To order a single copy write: Handbook Consumer Information Center, Pueblo, Colorado 81009 or order online at **www.pueblo.gsa.gov**

Savvy Shopper Habits

Compulsive buying and the urge to spend are best controlled by developing savvy shopping habits. To test your shopping habits, complete each of the 10 statements by using one of the phrases in the list on the next page. The answers are at the end of the quiz.

_____ 1. Clothing goes on sale

_____ 2. Shop

_____ 3. Decide how much money you have to spend, then

_____ 4. Shop when you are refreshed and not when

_____ 5. Avoid shopping

_____ 6. Use a shopping

_____ 7. Compare

_____ 8. Reduce the number of

_____ 9. Resist promotional tactics by

_____ 10. Find a substitute activity for

A. list.

B. shopping trips by planning ahead

C. towards the end of the season.

D. shopping, such as participating in an active sport or volunteering to help out at the local hospital.

E. alone. It is easier to say no to yourself than to a spouse or friend.

F. becoming familiar with prices before you shop.

G. aimlessly. Leave the store after you have made your purchases.

H. leave extra money, your checkbook, and credit cards at home.

I. before you buy.

J. you are tired, hungry, or rushed. Chances are you will not take time to compare prices, brands, or features, to try on clothing or test furniture.

Answers: 1c, 2e, 3h, 4j, 5g, 6a, 7i, 8b, 9f, 10d

So, the next time you go shopping, think about how you can be a more savvy shopper in order to make your shopping trip worth while, but also to only spend what you want to spend on items you want to buy.

Complaining Effectively

Complaining about products and services is important if there is a true reason to complain. It allows companies to fix or change the product or service to better meet the needs of all consumers. Thus, if you have a problem with a company, make your complaint known, or if you think the product does not live up to its sales claims, complain.

The first step is to discuss the problem with the seller. Calmly and accurately describe the problem and what action you want taken. **Keep a record** of your efforts to resolve the problem, but make sure to allow time for the person you contacted to resolve the problem. Then, do not give up if you are not satisfied. Keep pursuing the issue or problem up the chain of command if necessary. It is important to keep copies of any correspondence you have regarding your complaints, as well as all documentation you have about the product or service about which you are complaining.

One way to make a complaint is to write a letter to the seller, manufacturer, or service provider. The following is a template of a complaint letter that you can use as a guide to assist you in addressing your problem.

Complaint Letter Template

(*Your Address*)

(*Your City, State, ZIP Code*)

(*Date*)

(*Name of Contact Person, if available*)

(*Title, if available*)

(*Company Name*)

(*Consumer Complaint Division, if you have no contact person*)

(*Street Address*)

(*City, State, ZIP code*)

Dear (*Contact Person*):

Re: (*account number, if applicable*)

On (*date*), I (bought, leased, rented or had repaired) a (name of the product with serial or model number or service performed) at (location, date and other important details of the transaction).

> ➤ describe purchase
> ➤ name of product, serial numbers
> ➤ include date and place of purchase

Unfortunately, your product (*or service*) has not performed well (*or the service was inadequate*) because (*state the problem*). I am disappointed because (*explain the problem: for example, the product not does work properly, the service was not performed correctly; I was billed the wrong amount, something was not disclosed clearly or was misrepresented, etc.*).

➤ state problem

➤ give history

To resolve the problem, I would appreciate your (*state the specific action you want – money back, charge card credit, repair, exchange, etc.*). Enclosed are copies (*do not send originals*) of my records (*include receipts, guarantees, warranties, canceled checks, contracts, model and serial numbers, and any other documents*).

➤ ask for specific action

➤ enclose copies of documents

I look forward to your reply and a resolution to my problem, and I will wait until (*set a time limit*) before seeking help from a consumer protection agency or the Better Business Bureau. Please contact me at the above address or by phone at (*home and/or office numbers with area codes*).

➤ allow time for action

➤ state how you can be reached

Sincerely,

(*your name*)

Enclosure(s)

cc: (*reference to whom you are sending a copy of this letter, if anyone*)

After sending such a letter, if your problem is not remedied to your satisfaction, do not be afraid to take the further action you mentioned in your letter. You can complain to groups such as the Better Business Bureau, but there could also be a state or governmental regulatory board responsible for the products or services involved. If that is the case, you can make a complaint to the appropriate board. This would at least be a way to warn future consumers of your experience with this person or business.

In addition, many local television stations have consumer protection programs. Notifying the local media of the situation often times forces the person or business involved to try to solve your problem in order to avoid the bad publicity. In this situation, not only does your problem hopefully get resolved to your satisfaction, but you are also able to warn other consumers before the same thing happens to them.

RED FLAGS OF FRAUD

Consumer protection offices urge consumers to be aware of the red flags of fraud. Walk away from bogus offers. Toss out the junk mail and hang up when you hear the following:

- 🛒 "Sign up now or the price will increase"
- 🛒 "You have been specially selected ..."
- 🛒 "You have won..."
- 🛒 "All we need is your credit card (or bank account) number – for identification only"
- 🛒 "I just happen to have some leftover paving material from a job down the street..."
- 🛒 "Be your own boss! Never work for anyone else again. Just send in $50 for your supplies and..."

In addition, it is wise to stay away from telemarketers who want to:

- 🛒 Send a courier service to pick up money.
- 🛒 Have you wire funds.
- 🛒 Automatically withdraw money from your checking account.

⏢ Offer you a free prize but charge handling and shipping fees.

⏢ Ask for your credit card number, checking or savings account number, Social Security number, or other personal information.

⏢ Demand payment in advance especially for employment referrals, credit repair, or providing a loan or credit card.

How to Get Your Free Credit Report

The recently passed Fair Trade and Accurate Credit Transactions Act (FACT) requires that individuals be provided with a free credit report from each of the three major credit bureaus (Equifax, Trans Union, and Experian) once each year.

Due to a rapidly rising level of identity theft, consumers should check their reports annually. Knowing your credit score and how to improve it may be valuable if you plan to apply for credit in the near future. You can get your free credit report three ways.

⏢ Online – **www.annualcreditreport.com**

⏢ Phone – **877-322-8228.**

⏢ Mail – **Annual Credit Report Service P.O. Box 105281 Atlanta, GA 30348-5281.**

You should be aware that all three credit bureaus will try to sell you additional products, including your credit score.

If you find any errors in your report, let the consumer reporting company know in writing immediately. They must investigate the items in question and they usually do this within 30 days, unless they deem your dispute frivolous.

KEEPING GOOD RECORDS

Are you organized? Can you retrieve an important paper or receipt quickly? Do you have a system for keeping records?

Certain records provide proof of age, marriage, ownership, military service or other family events.

Some of these records you may only need two or three times. However, when you need them, you may only have a few hours, or possibly a few days, in which to locate them. This may sound like plenty of time, but the time you need the records is not the time to learn that you cannot remember where you put them or you no longer have them. Not to mention that it may take months to replace the records if you cannot find them. In addition to helping you find information quickly and providing security for hard to replace documents, a good record keeping system can also help you prove ownership in a lawsuit, inheritance dispute, or property fight, and can be used for a property settlement in a divorce.

To develop a good record keeping system, first you will need to determine what records need to be kept. Then, you and your family can decide where to keep, and develop any system needed to maintain those records. To get you started with developing your own system, here is a list of questions to ask yourself:

- ⏞ How easy or difficult is it for other family members to figure out your record system?

- ⏞ Who besides you knows how to find the needed information about family household assets and obligations?

- ⏞ Do I have a list of family advisors, such as bankers, financial planner, insurance representatives, employers, creditors, and debtors that my family will need?

Household Filing System

A household record keeping system does not need to be complex, but you want a system that is easy to use and designed for your specific needs. The system may be as elaborate as a home office or as simple as a drawer. You could consider purchasing a filing cabinet, but if you do not have much space you can buy accordion folders, a storage chest that fits under the bed, or use an appropriately sized cardboard box. In any event, it will be helpful to keep working files accessible, and then store permanent files in a secure space.

It does not matter who organizes your family's records, but it is probably best to use the talents of the person in your family with the best business sense or the best organizational skills. However, the entire family should understand the family's record keeping system, because cooperation from the entire family will allow you to work as a team to keep valuable documents organized.

Records that you might keep for your family at home, along with the time they should be kept, include:

Item	Amount of Time to Keep Record
Automobile title	During ownership
Appliance records (manuals, warranty cards, serial and model numbers)	During ownership and/or while warranty is in effect
Bank statements & cancelled checks	3-6 years if they are income tax related; otherwise, maintain while the account is open
Church records	Permanent records
Credit card information (including card number and toll-free number to call if lost or stolen)	Review annually and revise as necessary
Educational records (including transcripts, diplomas and certificates)	Permanent records

Item	Amount of Time to Keep Record
Employment records (such as resumes, recommendation letters, names and addresses of former employers and those willing to write recommendations, employee benefits, including health insurance)	Permanent records
Family and financial records (net worth statement – see below)	Update annually
Farm or business record books	Up to 6 years
Guarantees and warranties	During ownership and/or while warranty is in effect
Home improvement records	3-6 years if income tax related; while you own the property (can transfer copy to new owners upon sale of property)
Household inventory (copy)	Update annually

Item	Amount of Time to Keep Record
Income tax working records – current year	6 years to permanent, but move out of active files after the current year
Insurance policies	While in effect
Loan records	While in effect; 3-6 years if income tax related
Medical bills and insurance claims	Until paid in full (the exception is medical receipts if you are itemizing on your taxes or those you want to save as evidence of certain treatments; you should also keep a copy of health records, including shot records, prescriptions and x-rays)
Passports	(optional)
Property tax records	3-6 years if income tax related and/or permanent record
Receipts and receipted bills	During ownership; 3-6 years if income tax related

Item	Amount of Time to Keep Record
Retirement plans	While in effect
Safe deposit box inventory	Review annually and revise as necessary
Social Security card	Permanent record
Wills/letters of last instructions (copies)	While in effect (destroy old original and all copies if new estate planning documents are drafted)

Some records you can discard annually, and tax time is a good time to sort through your files and discard those records that you do not need to maintain. The records that can generally be discarded include the following:

⏜ Cancelled checks that are not needed for proof of purchase or income tax purposes (such as checks for groceries, clothing, monthly utility bills or cash)

⏜ Expired warranties

⏜ Receipts recorded in your account book (if they are not needed for resale or tax purposes.)

⏜ Records of appliances that have been replaced

➤ Sales slips recorded under the proper category in your account book

➤ Washing and cleaning instruction for fabrics and garments no longer used

Some Records Are Kept in Your Wallet

In addition to the home filing system, some records you will actually carry with you on a daily basis – in your wallet. Just because these records are not "filed" in the ordinary sense of the word, do not neglect their importance. Some of these records include:

➤ Credit cards

➤ Driver's license

➤ Identification cards

➤ Medical information

➤ Membership cards

➤ Person(s) to notify in case of an emergency

Although you may be tempted to carry your Social Security card in your wallet because there are times when you might need it for identification purposes, it is wise to leave it at home to prevent identify theft. In addition, if your state allows, you should replace your Social Security Number on your driver's license as another way to prevent identity theft.

Electronic Record Keeping

Buying a home computer just to organize and store important records and family information could be a questionable use of money. However, if you already own a computer, or have already decided to purchase one, you can certainly use the technology to get organized. There is software available on the market that will allow you to create a home inventory, pay bills, track monthly income and expenses, set up a budget, compute taxes, balance bank accounts, track stocks, bonds, and mutual funds, record your family's history and much more.

If you decide to use the computer for record keeping remember that your records will only be complete if you enter all of the information. Keeping up the data entry will take discipline; however, you will probably find that the results are worth the hassle.

You will also want to back up the information FREQUENTLY. This can be done onto some sort of disc or other media storage device compatible with your computer. Do not wait until you lose three or four months worth of data to learn this lesson.

Before buying your computer, printer, or software, ask friends, family, and merchants for their recommendations. Then, shop around (using your savvy shopping habits developed earlier) to find the products that best suit your needs.

Safe Deposit Box Inventory

Every family should consider renting a safe deposit box, or at the very least invest in a fire proof container that will withstand 1700 degrees Fahrenheit for one hour. You should also know the contents of your safe deposit box or fire proof container.

A safe deposit box is the best place to store documents or records which are difficult, time consuming, or expensive to replace. They are available at local banks or savings and loan associations. The rental charge depends on the size of the box and the fee structure of the institution. A good guide to the size of a safe deposit box is to select one that is large enough for your important papers yet small enough to keep out unnecessary items. The amount of storage space and the type of protection needed should also be taken into consideration.

Every family should have at least two copies of an inventory of the contents of their safe deposit box. One copy should be kept in the box, the other in your home filing system. Important papers to keep in your safe deposit box are the following:

- Adoption papers
- Automobile titles/bills of sale
- Birth, death and marriage certificates
- Church records
- Citizenship papers
- Contract papers
- Death certificates of close family members

- Divorce and separation papers
- Durable power of attorney
- Household inventory (original)
- Leases
- List of insurance policies
- Marriage certificate
- Military records
- Passports (optional)
- Patents and copyrights
- Property deeds and mortgage papers
- Savings and investment certificates (including savings bonds)
- Social Security card(s) (optional)
- Wills

Accessibility and the ability to replace documents should help you decide what to include in your safe deposit box. For example, you might keep the original copy of your will in a safe deposit box. If the safe deposit box is owned jointly, the co-owner will have access to the box after death, but if it is not owned jointly, your executor may have some initial difficulty accessing the contents of the box. Thus, if you choose to keep your original will in the safe deposit box, you should also keep a copy at home for reference purposes. As another example, savings bonds can be replaced without cost, but securing replacement bonds can take time. As a result, savings bonds are best kept in a safe deposit box. On the other hand, items that can be replaced rather easily do not need to be kept in a safe deposit box. Items in this category include copies of insurance policies because they can be obtained from your insurance company, and you can get cancelled checks from your bank (usually for a fee).

Because the ability to access the contents of your safe deposit box is important, you need to be sure to keep track of the key or other entry/access device. In addition, banks often declare that they are not liable for the contents of the safe deposit box, so it is especially important to keep the key in a safe location.

On the next page there is a worksheet to help you develop your family's safe deposit box inventory:

Your Valuable Family Papers Safe Deposit Box Inventory		
Location of Box		
Box Number		
Location of Keys		
Box in Names Of		
Item	Date Deposited	Date Removed

Social Security and Name Changes

It is important that the Social Security Administration have correct information about any name changes, which often occur when people marry. Make sure to report any name change to the Social Security as soon as possible after the name change becomes official. For people employed outside the home, reporting your name change assures that you will receive proper credit for your earnings. This is important because your earnings record determines your qualifications for benefits. For people who do not work outside the home, reporting the change will ensure that your Social Security record shows the correct name when it is time to apply for benefits.

It is also important for the IRS and Social Security records to show the same name and Social Security number. If they do not, any tax refund due to you may be delayed.

To report a name change, call toll-free, 1-800-772-1213, or visit your local Social Security office. You will need to complete an Application for a Social Security Card and provide proof of your name change. This proof could be in the form of a marriage certificate that verifies the old and new names, or it could be with two other documents showing the former and the new names. The application form lists acceptable documents, but keep in mind that all documents must be original or certified copies.

It is easy to do, and best of all, it is free. So, do not be misled by any business that offers to complete the paperwork for you – for a fee. The process is simple and you do not need to pay anyone to get you a revised Social Security card.

Income Tax Records

A common question is how long to keep income tax records. In most cases the Internal Revenue Service (IRS) has three (3) years to audit federal income tax returns. However, this three-year time period is calculated from the date filed or due or two years from the date the tax was paid, whichever date is later. In addition, if a taxpayer fails to report more than 25 percent of his or her reported gross income, the IRS has six (6) years to collect the tax or start legal proceedings, and if a taxpayer files a fraudulent or false tax return, with the intent to evade taxes, there is no limit on when the IRS completes an audit.

Below is a list that will help you determine what types of records to keep for tax purposes:

- ☙ Keep tax records a minimum of 3 years.
- ☙ Keep tax records 6 years if you think the IRS might question the amount of gross income reported.
- ☙ Keep receipts of major household items for insurance claims.
- ☙ Keep records of a home purchase and improvements as long as you own the property.
- ☙ Keep records of nondeductible Individual Retirement Accounts (IRA) contributions until all funds are withdrawn.
- ☙ Keep records of stocks, bonds, mutual funds, and annuity activity as long as you own the investments.

All receipts, statements, or other documentation used for income tax purposes can be kept with a particular year's income tax records. Those records should include all W-2s, 1099 forms, or any other IRS forms you receive for the certain tax year. Receipts are also important because the IRS does not accept a cancelled check as proof of payment. In addition, you may want to keep a copy of the year's bank statements to recall financial activity should you face an audit.

Assuming your financial activity is non-eventful, you can discard your tax records some time after seven (7) years. However, you may want to save any IRS Forms 8606, Nondeductible IRAs and Coverdell ESA's, you filed in the years when you made a nondeductible contribution to an IRA. These will be necessary if you ever need to justify why any portion of IRA withdrawals are not fully taxable.

Family Advisors

Every family needs an up-to-date list of family advisers. Such a list can save hours of searching and make it easier to cope with emergency situations. You should keep duplicate copies in your family's filing system for family records, and you can also keep a copy in your safe deposit box. In addition, at least one of your relatives or a trusted friend should also have a copy.

While creating the list is important, updating the list is equally as important. Having the list will not do you any good if the information on the list is not accurate. Make changes to the list throughout the year as any of the information changes, and then review the list at least annually to make sure the information is up-to-date. As noted earlier, tax time is a good time to discard the records you do not need to maintain, and it is also a good time to review your family advisors list.

Use this template to get you started in creating your own list:

Family Advisors		
Title	**Names & Address**	**Phone**
Accountant		
Attorney(s)		
Bank/ Banker(s)		

Family Advisors		
Title	Names & Address	Phone
Business Partner(s)		
Dentist		
Employer(s)		
Executor(s) of Wills		
Financial Planner		

Family Advisors		
Title	Names & Address	Phone
Insurance Agent(s)		
Physician(s)		
Religious Adviser		
Stock Broker(s)		

Family Advisors		
Title	**Names & Address**	**Phone**
Other Advisors		

Prepare Family Net Worth and Income Statements

The first step toward understanding your family's financial situation is to know your family's income. This can be especially important if your financial situation has changed, your income is irregular, or you plan to apply for a credit card or a loan.

To prepare an accurate income statement for your family, you will need to gather some information. You may be able to use last year's income tax records to estimate your current total income. However, you should also review paycheck stubs, broker statements, and checking account records. Recording this income information on check deposit forms can provide a back-up record. If you have to estimate some items of income, always under estimate the income in order to avoid future cash flow problems.

In addition to preparing an income statement for your family, you should also prepare a net worth statement. This is a statement that shows the difference between what you own (YOUR ASSETS) and what you owe (YOUR LIABILITIES). You can use it to measure the financial well-being of your family.

Preparing your family's net worth statement will:

- Assist you to determine your progress toward a financial goal.
- Provide you with a record of the value of your assets.
- Help you evaluate your investment, savings, and insurance needs.
- Enable you to spot trouble areas if your net worth is declining.
- Enable you to compare your financial positions at various time periods.
- Assist a lender to determine if you are credit-worthy.
- Help you decide if you can take on additional debt.

You should prepare your family's financial statement at the same time each year such as when you complete your income tax return. This will enable you to determine if your financial position is increasing or decreasing. If you have one or more retirement plans, are a homeowner, have personal savings or investments, or own a business, you may be surprised at how much you have!

Anytime you apply for credit, such as a home mortgage, a car loan, or a new credit card, creditors will examine your net worth statement carefully. A home mortgage lender will want to know how much long-term debt you have (car loans, alimony, child support and balances on charge cards which will take more than 10 months to pay off) and if a mortgage payments (principal and interest) plus real estate taxes and homeowners insurance on the house you want to buy will be more than 33% to 36% of your gross income. In addition, when you apply for a car loan, the lender will want to know if your long-term debt plus the new car loan will be less than 20% of your net income (gross income minus taxes and social security). Similarly, the credit card lender wants to know the outstanding balances on your current charge accounts and credit cards.

The first step to creating your net worth statement is to prepare a Financial Affairs Address Book. A good place to start in preparing this chart is your Financial Advisors list discussed above. In this chart, you will want to include more detailed information such as the names and addresses of your financial advisors, creditors, and investments, but also the account numbers. In the event you want to use this net worth statement to get a loan, lenders will use this information to verify the accuracy of your net worth statement.

Financial Affairs Address Book			
	Name	**Address**	**Account Number**
Banks			
Lenders			
Investments			

To prepare your net worth statement, create two lists: one for assets and one for liabilities.

Your assets will fall into three broad categories:

🎩 Cash on hand and other liquid assets – those which can easily be converted to cash.

➤ Cash on hand
➤ Cash in checking account
➤ Savings account balances

➤ Money market funds (Your last month's statement can give you an estimate of the value of your money market fund.)

➤ Life insurance, cash surrender value (Your insurance agent can give you the cash surrender value of each policy.)

⟋ Market value of investments – the value you would receive for an item if you had to sell it.

➤ Certificates of deposit

➤ Loans owed to you

➤ Savings bonds (The current cash value of a savings bond may be found on a table on the bond certificate.)

➤ Government securities (Call your broker to obtain the value of your investments that are not listed in the local media.)

➤ Municipal bonds (Call your broker to obtain the value of your investments that are not listed in the local media.)

➤ Common stock (An estimate of the current value of your stocks and bonds may be computed from the various quotations in the daily newspaper. Call your broker for investments not listed in the newspaper.)

➤ Corporate bonds (An estimate of the current value of your stocks and bonds may be computed from the various quotations in the daily newspaper. Call your broker for investments not listed in the newspaper.)

- ➤ Mutual funds (Periodic reports can give you an estimate of the value of your money market fund.)
- ➤ Annuities, current values (Periodic reports will give you the vested value of your retirement plan.)
- ➤ IRA accounts (Periodic reports will give you the vested value of your retirement plan.)
- ➤ Vested retirement plans, current values (Periodic reports from your employer will give you the vested value of your retirement plan.)
- ➤ Ownership in a business, current value
- ➤ Ownership in real estate, market value

≈ Personal and family assets (using a conservative market value estimate should you be forced to sell.)

- ➤ Home(s) (The price of the most recently sold house in your neighborhood can give you an estimated value of your home.)
- ➤ Household furnishings
- ➤ Personal items (jewelry, art, etc.) (Retailers or appraisers can provide you with estimated values of jewelry and collections.)
- ➤ Automobile(s) (An insurance agent can give you the blue book value of your car.)
- ➤ Appliances

➤ Collectables (antiques, coin or stamp collections, etc.) (Retailers or appraisers can provide you with estimated values of your collectables.)

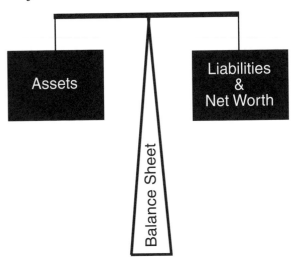

Your list of liabilities will reflect today's dollar value of what you owe to creditors. Check your latest balance(s) for the most up-to-date figures. The list of liabilities on your net worth statement should include items such as the following:

🪖 Mortgage debt – home(s)

🪖 Mortgage debt – other real estate

🪖 Personal loans

🪖 Business loans

🪖 Medical and other current bills

🪖 Taxes due

🪖 Car loan(s)

⬟ Credit card and charge account balances
⬟ School loans

Once you have prepared your list of assets and your list of liabilities, you can compare your assets to your liabilities. This process will allow to better understand your family's financial situation, and you can also use this net worth statement to make future plans with regard to your financial position, whether that be a decision to make different investment decisions to meet the diversification goals discussed above or a decision to pay off some debt.

Use the template at the end of this chapter on record keeping to set up your family's net worth statement.

Test Yourself

Now test your knowledge of family record keeping. One the next page are ten (10) TRUE or FALSE statements about important family records. Decide which statements are TRUE and place a "T" in the blank, and place an "F" in the blank if the statement is FALSE. Then, check your answers using the key at the bottom.

True or False	Statement
	1. Records are necessary to prove age, marriage, ownership, military service or other family changes.
	2. A safe deposit box is too expensive and unnecessary for a married couple.
	3. A home filing system begins with elaborate and expensive equipment.
	4. Every family should determine what records are valuable and where they should be stored.
	5. A list of family advisors such as bankers, insurance agents, physicians and attorneys is really not necessary.
	6. Banks are not liable for the contents of a safe deposit box.
	7. A safe deposit box should contain marriage and birth certificates, leases, list of insurance policies, bank statements, receipts and loan records.
	8. To replace a lost Social Security card, contact the local post office.
	9. To inquire about property and personal tax papers, contact the county tax collector's office.
	10. The family net worth statement helps you assess your family's financial status.

Answers: 1. True 2. False 3. False 4. True 5. False 6. True 7. False 8. False 9. True 10. True

Assets	
Cash on hand and other liquid assets	
Cash on hand	_____
Cash in checking account	_____
Savings account balances	_____
Money market funds	_____
Life insurance, cash surrender value	_____
Market value of investments	
Certificates of deposit	_____
Loans owed to you	_____
Savings bonds	_____
Government securities	_____
Municipal bonds	_____
Common stock	_____
Corporate bonds	_____
Mutual funds	_____
Annuities, current values	_____
IRA accounts	_____
Vested retirement plans, current values	_____
Ownership in a business	_____
Ownership in real estate	_____
Personal and family assets	
Home(s)	_____
Household furnishings	_____
Personal items	_____
Automobiles	_____
Appliances	_____
Collectibles	_____
Total	_____

Liabilities	
Mortgage debt – home(s)	_____
Mortgage debt – other real estate	_____
Personal loans	_____
Business loans	_____
Medical and other current bills	_____
Taxes due	_____
Car loans	_____
Credit card and charge account balances	_____
School loans	_____
Total	_____

Ultimately, with regard to your family's records, you should complete the items on the list below, and check each task when finished.

✔ When Complete	Getting Organized To Do List
	Set up a home filing system.
	Rent a safe deposit box to store important papers. Complete a Safe Deposit Box Inventory (see worksheet below).
	Complete your family net worth statement.
	Complete the chart on the Location of Important papers.
	Complete the chart on Family Advisors.
	Complete a Household Inventory.
	Keep your relatives informed.

Once these steps are completed, you will be well on your way to an organized household.

CONCLUSION

As you can see, there are many parts to a successful retirement. Many of the decisions made during the younger years can affect the long-term safety of your retirement income.

It is never too early or too late to take steps necessary to ensure that your money is safe and in the right place. Be warned, there are many out there who call themselves "Advisors" and claim to be looking after you, when in reality, they are looking after their own portfolio. Be careful about accepting advice from unknown sources. Use vigilance to discover the hidden fees, expenses, and commissions that directly affect not only your investment return but also the actual return of your investment.

Use common sense when it comes to your retirement accounts. Evaporation of your balance caused by an unscrupulous broker who has positioned you in an account infested with fees, risks, and commissions actually only benefits the person who sold you the account.

In addition, alarm bells should sound if you hear:

"Don't worry it's just a paper loss."

In some cases, this is the only time you have been able to get anything close to the truth from your Advisor. They are right, it IS a paper loss and that paper is green with pictures of Presidents on it.

Why is it that it always seems in life that the ones who tell you not to worry are usually the ones who put you in that particular situation to begin with?

This book was written to be used as a basic outline to help you understand the total picture of a true financial plan. As is my motto, it is always better to be prepared than to be surprised. The worst time to discover that you were doing something wrong is after the event has happened.

Growing up as a curious youngster who stuck my fingers in more than one electrical socket, I still remember my grandfather telling me:

"Pete, life is a learning experience and you will learn new things everyday but remember... a smart person learns from their mistakes while a genius learns from mistakes others make."

Let the mistakes of the past shape your future into a beaming legacy for future generations.

Wishing you all the best during the remainder of your Financial Safari!

ABOUT THE AUTHOR

Peter J. D'Arruda (Shown with his wife Kimberley and their 3 "children" Allie, Chelsey, and Penny) is a Certified Senior Advisor, Certified Estate Advisor, Certified Charitable Advisor, and Certified Annuity Consultant, Economist and No-

tary. He is a well known educator in the Atlantic Coast Region. For over 15 years Mr. D'Arruda has been teaching investors 50 and older how to preserve their assets, increase their income, and reduce income taxes.

Peter and Kimberley are proud parents of their first child, Caroline, who was born in September 2005, much to the delight of both of their parents who have been waiting patiently for a real grandchild.

Thousands have used Mr. D'Arruda's advice to wisely invest millions, to help reduce taxes while growing their assets, and to shield their valuable estates from estate taxes, probate, stock market losses, and the nursing home. Consequently, Mr.

D'Arruda is regarded as a local expert in the financial risks and opportunities of retirement. The son of educators, he is founder of the FINANCIAL SAFARI retirement planning seminar series seen in many North Carolina, South Carolina, and Virginia towns. Why not have him come speak with your civic or church group today? There is no cost and he even supplies a meal.

Mr. D'Arruda graduated from The University of North Carolina in 1988. He is a proud member of the local Chamber of Commerce, the National Council on Aging, the Better Business Bureau, and is recognized by the National Ethics Bureau (ethicscheck.com) with their highest ranking of A+ SUPERIOR. His main goal is to help seniors enjoy a financially secure, worry-free retirement.